The Fringe Benefits of Failure and
the Importance of Imagination

J.K. ROWLING

LITTLE, BROWN AND COMPANY

New York   Boston   London

Little, Brown and Company
Hachette Book Group
1290 Avenue of the Americas, New York, NY 10104
littlebrown.com

First Edition: April 2015
Published simultaneously in Great Britain by Little, Brown Book Group.

Little, Brown and Company is a division of Hachette Book Group, Inc. The Little, Brown name and logo are trademarks of Hachette Book Group, Inc.

The publisher is not responsible for websites (or their content) that are not owned by the publisher.

The Hachette Speakers Bureau provides a wide range of authors for speaking events. To find out more, go to hachettespeakersbureau.com or call (866) 376-6591.

Book design by Mario J. Pulice
Illustrations by Joel Holland, © 2015 by Little, Brown and Company

ISBN 978-0-316-36915-2
LCCN 2014959607

10 9 8 7 6 5 4 3 2 1

RRD-C

Printed in the United States of America

VERY GOOD LIVES

President Faust, members of the Harvard Corporation and the Board of Overseers, members of the faculty, proud parents, and, above all, graduates.

The first thing I would like to say is "thank you." Not only has Harvard given me an extraordinary honor, but the weeks of fear and nausea I have endured at the thought of giving this commencement address have made me lose weight. A win-win situation! Now all I have to do is take deep breaths, squint at the red banners, and convince myself that I am at the world's largest Gryffindor reunion.

Delivering a commencement address is a great responsibility, or so I thought until I cast my mind back to my own graduation. The commencement speaker that day was the distinguished British philosopher Baroness Mary Warnock. Reflecting on her speech has helped me enormously in writing this one,

because it turns out that I can't remember a single word she said. This liberating discovery enables me to proceed without any fear that I might inadvertently influence you to abandon promising careers in business, the law, or politics for the giddy delights of becoming a gay wizard.

You see? If all you remember in years to come is the "gay wizard" joke, I've come out ahead of Baroness Mary Warnock. Achievable goals: the first step to self-improvement.

Actually, I have racked my mind and heart for what I ought to say to you today. I have asked myself what I wish I had known at my own graduation, and what important lessons I have learned in the twenty-one years that have expired between that day and this.

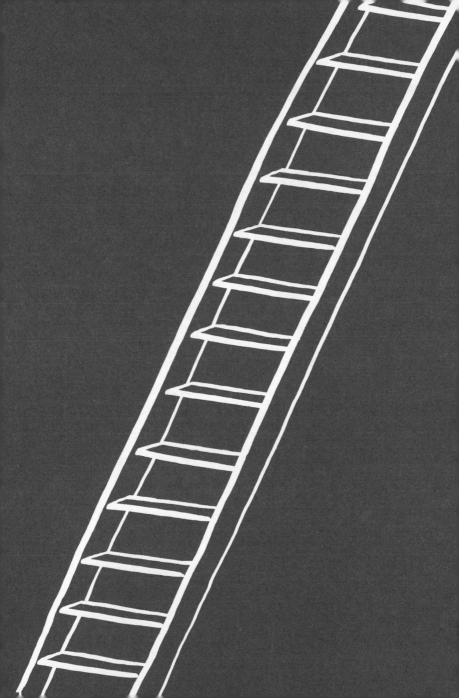

I have come up with two answers. On this wonderful day when we are gathered together to celebrate your academic success, I have decided to talk to you about the benefits of failure. And as you stand on the threshold of what is sometimes called "real life," I want to extol the crucial importance of imagination.

These may seem quixotic or paradoxical choices, but please bear with me.

Looking back at the twenty-one-year-old that I was at graduation is a slightly uncomfortable experience for the forty-two-year-old that she has become. Half my lifetime ago, I was striking an uneasy balance between the ambition I had for myself and what those closest to me expected of me.

I was convinced that the only thing I wanted to do, ever, was write novels. However, my parents, both of whom came from impoverished backgrounds and neither of whom had been to college, took the view that my overactive imagination was an amusing personal quirk that would never pay a mortgage or secure a pension. I know that the irony strikes with the force of a cartoon anvil now.

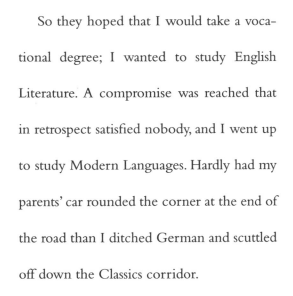

So they hoped that I would take a vocational degree; I wanted to study English Literature. A compromise was reached that in retrospect satisfied nobody, and I went up to study Modern Languages. Hardly had my parents' car rounded the corner at the end of the road than I ditched German and scuttled off down the Classics corridor.

I cannot remember telling my parents that I was studying Classics; they might well have found out for the first time on graduation day. Of all the subjects on this planet, I think they would have been hard put to name one less useful than Greek mythology when it came to securing the keys to an executive bathroom.

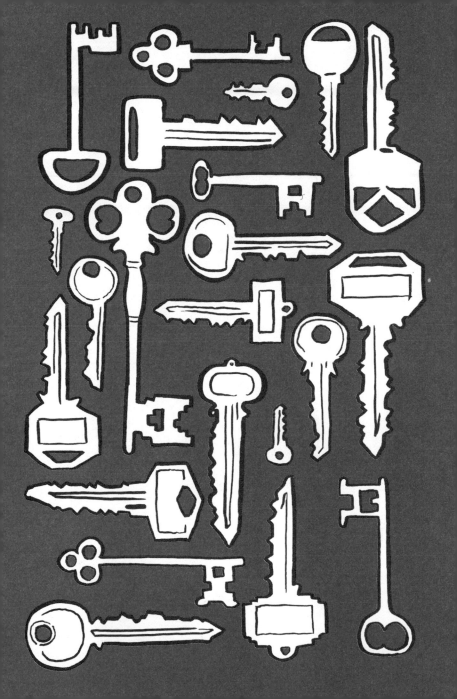

I would like to make it clear, in paren-
thesis, that I do not blame my parents for
their point of view. There is an expiration
date on blaming your parents for steering
you in the wrong direction; the moment
you are old enough to take the wheel,
responsibility lies with you. What is more, I
cannot criticize my parents for hoping that I
would never experience poverty. They had

been poor themselves, and I have since been poor, and I quite agree with them that it is not an ennobling experience. Poverty entails fear, and stress, and sometimes depression; it means a thousand petty humiliations and hardships. Climbing out of poverty by your own efforts—that is something on which to pride yourself, but poverty itself is romanticized only by fools.

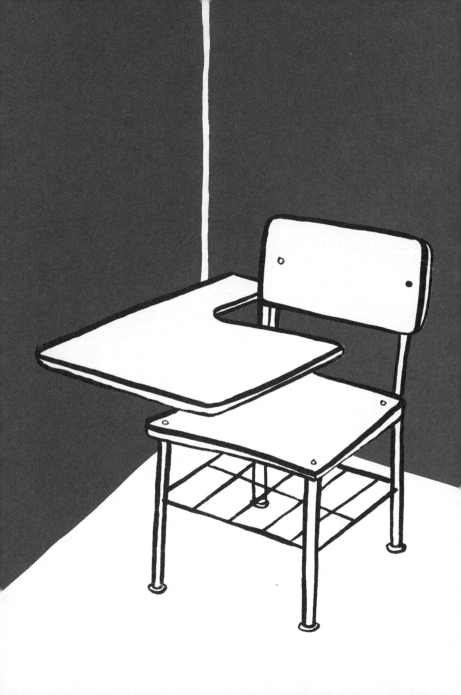

What I feared most for myself at your age was not poverty but failure.

At your age, in spite of a distinct lack of motivation at university, where I had spent far too long in the coffee bar writing stories and far too little time at lectures, I had a knack for passing examinations, and that, for years, had been the measure of success in my life and that of my peers.

I am not dull enough to suppose that because you are young, gifted, and well-educated, you have never known hardship or heartache. Talent and intelligence never yet inoculated anyone against the caprice of

the Fates, and I do not for a moment suppose

that everyone here has enjoyed an existence of

unruffled privilege and contentment.

However, the fact that you are graduating from Harvard suggests that you are not very well acquainted with failure. You might be driven by a fear of failure quite as much as a desire for success. Indeed, your conception of failure might not be too far removed from the average person's idea of success, so high have you already flown.

"I was the biggest failure I knew"

Ultimately we all have to decide for ourselves what constitutes failure, but the world is quite eager to give you a set of criteria, if you let it. So I think it fair to say that by any conventional measure, a mere seven years after my graduation day, I had failed on an epic scale. An exceptionally short-lived marriage had imploded, and I was jobless, a lone parent, and as poor as it is possible to be in modern Britain without being homeless. The fears that my parents had had for me, and that I had had for myself, had both come to pass, and by every usual standard I was the biggest failure I knew.

Now, I am not going to stand here and tell you that failure is fun. That period of my life was a dark one, and I had no idea that there was going to be what the press has since represented as a kind of fairy-tale resolution. I had no idea then how far the tunnel extended, and for a long time any light at the end of it was a hope rather than a reality.

So why do I talk about the benefits of failure? Simply because failure meant a stripping away of the inessential. I stopped pretending to myself that I was anything other than what I was and began to direct all my energy into finishing the only work that mattered to me. Had I really succeeded at anything else, I might never have found

the determination to succeed in the one arena where I believed I truly belonged. I was set free, because my greatest fear had been realized, and I was still alive, and I still had a daughter whom I adored, and I had an old typewriter and a big idea. And so rock bottom became the solid foundation on which I rebuilt my life.

You might never fail on the scale I did, but some failure in life is inevitable. It is impossible to live without failing at something, unless you live so cautiously that you might as well not have lived at all—in which case, you fail by default.

Failure gave me an inner security that I had never attained by passing examinations. Failure taught me things about myself that I could have learned no other way. I discovered that I had a strong will and more discipline than I had suspected; I also found out that I had friends whose value was truly above the price of rubies.

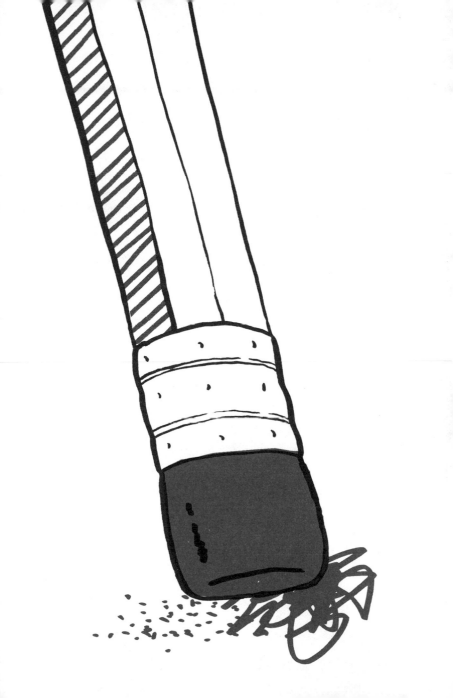

The knowledge that you have emerged wiser and stronger from setbacks means that you are, ever after, secure in your ability to survive. You will never truly know yourself, or the strength of your relationships, until both have been tested by adversity. Such knowledge is a true gift, for all that it is painfully won, and it has been worth more than any qualification I've ever earned.

humility

So given a Time-Turner, I would tell my twenty-one-year-old self that personal happiness lies in knowing that life is not a checklist of acquisition or achievement. Your qualifications, your CV, are not your life, though you will meet many people of my age and older who confuse the two. Life is difficult, and complicated, and beyond anyone's total control, and the humility to know that will enable you to survive its vicissitudes.

Now you might think that I chose my second theme, the importance of imagination, because of the part it played in rebuilding my life, but that is not wholly so. Though I personally will defend the value of bedtime stories to my last gasp, I have learned to value imagination in a much broader sense. Imagination is not only the uniquely human capacity to envision that which is not, and therefore the fount of all invention and innovation; in its arguably most transformative and revelatory capacity, it is the power that enables us to empathize with humans whose experiences we have never shared.

One of the greatest formative experiences of my life preceded Harry Potter, though it informed much of what I subsequently wrote in those books. This revelation came in the form of one of my earliest day jobs. Though I was sloping off to write stories during my lunch hours, I paid the rent in my early twenties by working at the African research department of Amnesty International's head-quarters in London.

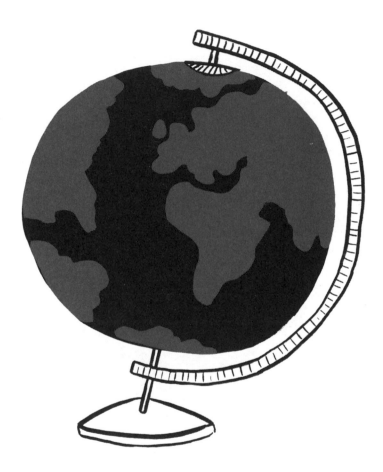

There in my little office I read hastily scribbled letters smuggled out of totalitarian regimes by men and women who were risking imprisonment to inform the outside world of what was happening to them. I saw photographs of those who had disappeared without a trace, sent to Amnesty by their desperate families and friends. I read the testimony of torture victims and saw pictures of their injuries. I opened handwritten eyewitness accounts of summary trials and executions, of kidnappings and rapes.

Many of my coworkers were ex–political prisoners, people who had been displaced from their homes or fled into exile because they had the temerity to speak against their governments. Visitors to our offices included those who had come to give information, or to try to find out what had happened to those they had left behind.

I shall never forget the African torture victim, a young man no older than I was at the time, who had become mentally ill after all he had endured in his homeland. He trembled uncontrollably as he spoke into a video camera about the brutality inflicted upon him. He was a foot taller

than I was and seemed as fragile as a child.

I was given the job of escorting him back

to the Underground station afterward,

and this man whose life had been shat-

tered by cruelty took my hand with ex-

quisite courtesy and wished me future

happiness.

A
SCREAM
OF
PAIN
AND
HORROR

And as long as I live I shall remember walking along an empty corridor and suddenly hearing, from behind a closed door, a scream of pain and horror such as I have never heard since. The door opened, and the researcher poked out her head and told me to run and make a hot drink for the young man sitting with her. She had just had to give him the news that, in retaliation for his own outspokenness against his country's regime, his mother had been seized and executed.

Every day of my working week in my early twenties, I was reminded how incredibly fortunate I was to live in a country with a democratically elected government, where legal representation and a public trial were the rights of everyone.

Every day, I saw more evidence of the evils humankind will inflict on their fellow humans to gain or maintain power. I began to have nightmares, literal nightmares, about some of the things I saw, heard, and read.

And yet I also learned more about human goodness at Amnesty International than I had ever known before.

Amnesty mobilizes thousands of people who have never been tortured or imprisoned for their beliefs to act on behalf of those who have. The power of human empathy leading to collective action saves lives and frees prisoners. Ordinary people, whose personal well-being and security are assured, join together in huge numbers to save people they do not know and will never meet. My small participation in that process was one of the most humbling and inspiring experiences of my life.

Unlike any other creature on this planet, human beings can learn and understand without having experienced. They can think themselves into other people's places.

Of course, this is a power, like my brand of fictional magic, that is morally neutral. One might use such an ability to manipulate or control just as much as to understand or sympathize.

"They can think themselves into other people's places"

"They can refuse to know"

And many prefer not to exercise their imaginations at all. They choose to remain comfortably within the bounds of their own experience, never troubling to wonder how it would feel to have been born other than they are. They can refuse to hear screams or to peer inside cages; they can close their minds and hearts to any suffering that does not touch them personally; they can refuse to know.

I might be tempted to envy people who can live that way, except that I do not think they have any fewer nightmares than I do. Choosing to live in narrow spaces leads to a form of mental agoraphobia, and that brings its own terrors. I think the willfully

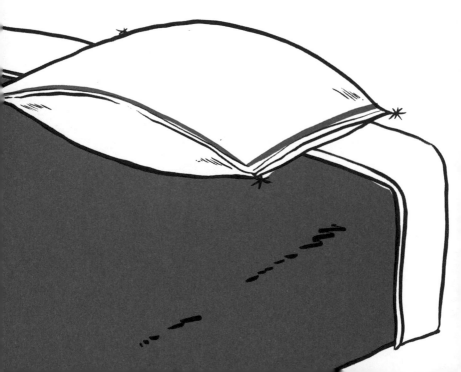

unimaginative see more monsters. They are often more afraid.

What is more, those who choose not to empathize enable real monsters. For without ever committing an act of outright evil ourselves, we collude with it through our own apathy.

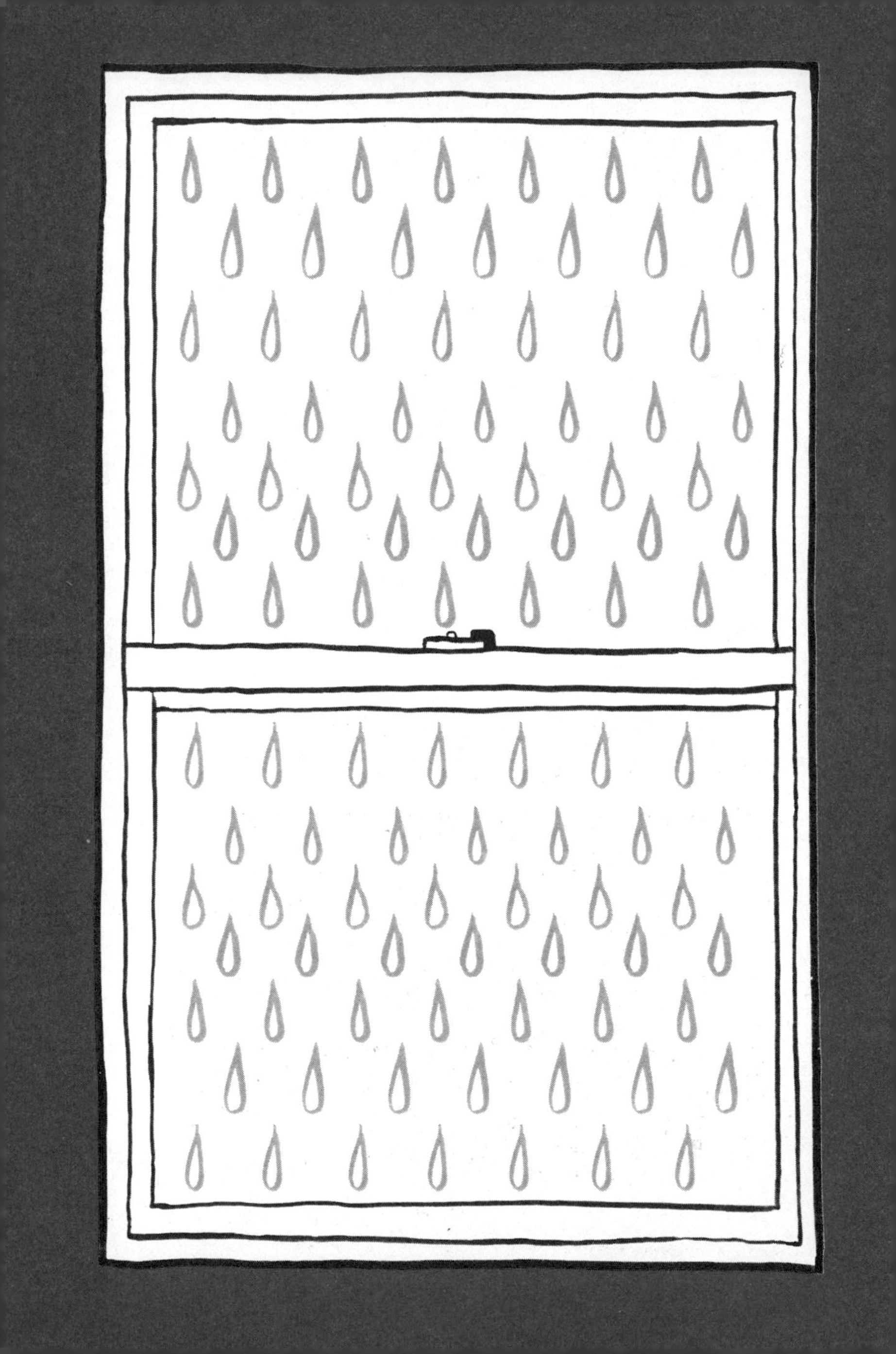

One of the many things I learned at the end of that Classics corridor, down which I ventured at the age of eighteen in search of something I could not then define, was this, written by the Greek author Plutarch: "What we achieve inwardly will change outer reality."

That is an astonishing statement, and yet proven a thousand times every day of our lives. It expresses, in part, our inescapable connection with the outside world, the fact that we touch other people's lives simply by existing.

But how much more are you, Harvard graduates of 2008, likely to touch other people's lives? Your intelligence, your capacity for hard work, the education you have earned and received, give you unique status and unique responsibilities. Even your nationality sets you apart. The great majority of you belong to the world's only remaining superpower. The way you vote, the way you live, the way you protest, the pressure you bring to bear on your government, has an impact way beyond your borders. That is your privilege, and your burden.

If you choose to use your status and influence to raise your voice on behalf of those who have no voice; if you choose to identify not only with the powerful but with the powerless; if you retain the ability to imagine yourself into the lives of those who do not have your advantages, then it will not only be your proud families who celebrate your existence but thousands and millions of people whose reality you have helped change. We do not need magic to transform our world; we carry all the power we need inside ourselves already: we have the power to imagine better.

I am nearly finished. I have one last hope for you, which is something that I already had at twenty-one. The friends with whom I sat on graduation day have been my friends for life. They are my children's godparents, the people to whom I've been able to turn in times of real trouble, people who have been kind enough not to sue me when I took their names for Death Eaters. At our graduation we were bound by enormous affection, by our shared experience of a time that could never come again, and, of course, by the knowledge that we held certain photographic evidence that would be exceptionally valuable if any of us ran for prime minister.

So today, I wish you nothing better than similar friendships. And tomorrow, I hope that even if you remember not a single word of mine, you remember those of Seneca, another of those old Romans I met when I fled down the Classics corridor in retreat from career ladders, in search of ancient wisdom:

"As is a tale, so is life: not how long it is, but how good it is, is what matters."

I wish you all very good lives. Thank you very much.

About the Author

J.K. Rowling is the author of the bestselling Harry Potter series of seven books, published between 1997 and 2007, which have sold over 450 million copies worldwide, are distributed in more than 200 territories, are translated into 78 languages, and have been turned into eight blockbuster films. Her first novel for adult readers, *The Casual Vacancy*, was published in September 2012 and her first two crime novels, written under the pseudonym

Robert Galbraith, were published in 2013 and 2014 respectively.

As well as receiving an OBE for services to children's literature, J.K. Rowling supports a number of causes through her charitable trust, Volant. She is also the founder and president of the children's charity Lumos, which works to end the institutionalization of children globally and ensure all children grow up in a safe and caring environment.